Coveralls
& Tell-Alls

EVERYTHING YOU NEED TO KNOW ABOUT LEADERSHIP I LEARNED ON THE FARM

Sheila Webb Pierson

INDIE BOOKS
INTERNATIONAL

No part of this publication may be reproduced or distributed in any form
or by any means without the prior permission of the publisher. Requests
for permission should be directed to permissions@indiebooksintl.com, or
mailed to Permissions, Indie Books International, 2424 Vista Way, Suite 316,
Oceanside, CA 92054.

Neither the publisher nor the author is engaged in rendering legal or other
professional services through this book. If expert assistance is required, the
services of appropriate professionals should be sought. The publisher and
the author shall have neither liability nor responsibility to any person or
entity with respect to any loss or damage caused directly or indirectly by the
information in this publication.

ISBN-10: 1-941870-60-0
ISBN-13: 978-1-941870-60-0
Library of Congress Control Number: 2016940255

Designed by Joni McPherson, mcphersongraphics.com

INDIE BOOKS INTERNATIONAL, LLC
2424 VISTA WAY, SUITE 316
OCEANSIDE, CA 92054
www.indiebooksintl.com

To my dad, Dwayne Webb,
I dedicate this book to your precious memory.

Whether or not I fully understood at the time it was imparted, your infallible wisdom has been profound at all stages of my life. The dedication and incomparable passion you brought to agriculture and the people business continue to encourage and inspire me, especially at times when I struggle to find my own passion. Your unfailing love bestowed so generously upon your family and treasured members of the community is overwhelming even now, and you remain a model to anyone who seeks a model for how to live.

You found your passion, you lived your passion, and your passion lives on within us.

Let's just say it's "better than cherry pie and ice cream."

To my cousin, Jeff,
I dedicate chapter 3 to your memory.

Goodness, the stories I could tell about our adventures growing up in this family. Granted, some tales are sworn to secrecy and will remain that way until I forget our vows of silence or the statutes of limitations are lifted, either of which could happen at any time. What a blessing it is to have traveled our journey of youth together—I wouldn't trade it for the world. You taught me to embrace the unknown, as you truly understood nothing on a farm but didn't seem to care.

Thank you for the memories.

Contents

CHAPTER 1

My Gateway Crime

Frozen in fear, I stood silently staring down the barrel of a pistol. While not sure what kind of pistol, I clearly recognized it was a gun. The make and model seemed a bit unimportant at this moment in time.

The police officer holding the gun was intense. He screamed at me, "Get down! Get down!"

How does someone who is teaching a business training class find herself in such a predicament? A million questions flashed through my head but the most daunting one was: "Where did my life of crime start?"

I am just a simple farm girl from the Ozarks. Was this going to be the legacy that I leave? *Seriously*, I have college degrees in agriculture.

Actually, this book is not about my life of crime, but what I have learned about leadership. In the corporate world, we are taught that leadership is all about influence:

Influence = Strength + Intelligence
+ Go-To Person + Communication Skills

Based on that model and my early escapades in my corporate career, becoming influential seemed a bit out of reach for someone like me.

I have noticed through the years that a different model is actually more effective. Interestingly enough, it is the same model my dad taught me from the farm:

Influence = Be Proud of Where You Came From
+ Admit Mistakes + Communicate
+ Laugh at Yourself + Serve Others

This, ladies and gentlemen, is a collection of confessions that will explain everything you need to know about leadership. I promise.

 # CHAPTER 2

Be Proud of Where You Come From

I was born in Arkansas and raised on a small dairy farm. Everything I needed to know about leadership I learned on the farm. Or, should I say, I learned from a farmer.

I was fortunate to have a close family and be blessed with good parents. Growing up on a farm isn't glamorous. Oh no; farm life is not like living in a rustic log house, doing chores two hours a day, and then reading a newspaper on the front porch with a perfectly groomed collie resting peacefully under your feet. Television has missed reality just a tad. If you want a reality show that is the real deal, try farming for a living.

We lived in a small but modern red brick house on 120 rolling acres in the Ozarks straddling the

Arkansas-Oklahoma border. Again, film and TV will always paint a picture of a green, grassy knoll. Northwest Arkansas, where our farm resided, is far from that. Grassy yes, for about four months out of the year. We were lucky to be able to experience all four seasons. On rare occasions (not really that rare) we could experience all four in one day. Yep, that is true.

Our farm was unique in that we had meadows, a wooded area with wildlife, hay fields, and a cemetery. The cemetery was not ours or even reserved for our family. It belonged to another family. However, the cemetery added a value for me as I was growing up. There is nothing better for a fall party than playing hide-and-seek in the dark through an overgrown cemetery. Maybe that is why I enjoy Halloween so much.

We had many barns, one of which was our dairy barn. Our dairy barn was moderately modern as well. A dairy barn is basically a cement brick building housing two main compartments. The first is the area where we milked the cows.

For our enterprise, the cows were ushered into one of two sides of this first area. Each side had room for six cows at a time. This meant we could milk twelve cows at once. Each station had a stainless steel bowl that held grain so the cows could eat while we attached the milkers.

In the middle of the two aisles of cows was a pit, an alley of sorts. That is where I spent what turned out to be years of my life. It wasn't glamorous, but it was noble and important work. We made certain each cow had grain in her bowl; we washed her udder, attached the milker, and then removed everything when she was empty.

The other compartment was our milk room. Once the milk left the cow, it traveled in a maze of stainless steel pipes to the milk room and landed in a giant tank. That tank housed the milk at a controlled temperature until a tanker truck came to empty it.

Our milk truck driver's name was Charlie, and he came every other day. He was about six feet four inches, 180 pounds, and always had a grin on his face. Visiting with Charlie was always a bright spot in the day.

Charlie always had the gossip. Living and working on a farm sometimes limited our ability to properly interact with our neighbors, so we were always starved for good gossip. For instance, Randy and Kate were getting a divorce. Randy had chickens as well as dairy cattle. According to Charlie, that became a little too mundane for Kate. My mother, Charlotte Webb—yes, I'm serious, that is her name, so she went by Janie—told Charlie, "Kate was just too pretty for Randy," then grinned with this compassionate smirk. My mother always liked to sugarcoat things. That, my friends, is sarcasm. My mother is blunt and can never understand why people get their feelings hurt. "People are just too sensitive anymore," she was always saying.

I think most people have this view of us Southern women as being genteel, matronly belles who dress to the nines and often need naps due to our delicate natures. Scarlett O'Hara we are not. I was born into a family of very strong Southern women as role models. My mother's mother, Grandma Jessie, was raised in Shawnee, Oklahoma during The Dust Bowl. And she survived. She was a "Rosie the Riveter" in World War II. What that translated to was a very independent woman who never feared sharing an opinion. Let me assure you, Grandma Jessie's opinion was the only one that mattered. If she wanted to express an opinion, then I needed to listen. But I always felt she earned that right. Remember, she was a survivor.

My mother was innately very similar. We did have our rules of hospitality. So, as blunt as my matriarchal society was, it was imperative we always said it with a smile, to soften the blow, or more likely, to just confuse our audience. It can really be a vernacular talent to insult and compliment someone in the very same breath—a talent that only works for the women of the South, not the men.

We had three or four John Deere tractors. My father was an avid John Deere fan. But despite his loyalty to the green machines, seldom did more than one tractor work at any given time. Of course, that just depends on your definition of "working tractor." My dad loved to tinker with his tractors. In fact, he restored a John Deere Model M that he would later drive in parades and allow my children to steer.

We raised Guernsey cows with a sprinkle of other breeds like Holstein, Jersey, and even Brown Swiss. However, Guernsey was the special breed to my father. He became a world-renowned breeder.

My chore each day was caring for the babies. Newborn dairy calves appear to be cute. You might even consider them to be adorable. But let me tell you, *nothing* could be farther from the truth. They were like little demons. Dairy product companies like Kraft and Borden portray them in their advertisements as helpless creatures running and grazing through beautiful green meadows. Their pictures of dairy calves almost had them smiling. Some of them even talk in the television commercial. Here's the fact you need to know about these fuzzy brown and white critters: calves don't smile. The only time ours showed me their teeth was before they tried to take a bite out of me.

The truth is these calves are waiting—maybe even plotting in baby cow tongue—to attack you. I was responsible for feeding each calf one bottle full of milk each morning around 6:00 a.m. I know what you are thinking—how fun. Just like a petting zoo. Hardly.

The newborns were tough. There is no coaxing a hungry calf. It runs from you, kicks at you, and lays down in a retreat mode, but will not drink milk from a bottle. They slam their little jaws tight like crocodile jaws. Trying to get their mouths open so they can taste fresh milk is next to impossible. Even when I could get the nipple past their lips, the resistance kicked in. They would stare at me with those giant solid brown eyes squinting stubbornly, as if they were plotting their next move. It was a battle of the wits. Apparently I didn't have much wit, because I frequently needed my dad's help.

The older calves were almost as bad once they became accustomed to my bringing food. They impatiently waited for breakfast or supper by kicking and running in their pens. They would go crazy the second I dropped the bottle over the fence and latched it to the gate. They would drink their milk in seconds and then demand more.

On occasion, they butted their bottle right out of the holder. This left me with the unenviable task of retrieving it. I would climb over the fence because we never had gates on hinges. All our fence sections were tied together with baling twine or wire. Once I was within reach of the calf, I was met with a hungry mouth pulling at any piece of clothing it could grab. As soon as my feet hit the hay floor, the calves would run and butt me in the stomach, side, backside—anywhere to get my attention.

The message was clear: "I want more. Moooooore!"

I sometimes had nightmares of a pen full of baby Guernseys attacking me. Like someone drowning in water, the last thing you would see is my hand in a desperate motion for help. That would be me under a sea of hungry Guernsey calves.

This happened twice a day, every single day of my young life. Before school and after school. I was always jealous of my friends who didn't have any chores. I wondered what it was like to just get up and go to school. If I ever complained, my dad would always say, "You are learning every day from your chores. How lucky are you?" Lucky, really?

Summer brought my most dreaded chore—hauling hay. Obviously, storing hay was critical for those long winter months. After the fields of grass died in late fall, hay and grain made up the cows' winter diet. It didn't matter how important hay was; I dreaded every moment of the process.

So did my brother, Lonnie, who was two years older than me. Lonnie was not a fit for farming. He was a fan of Doctor Who and was devoted to Atari. He was the only person I knew who wore a fifteen-foot crocheted scarf in July (see "fan of Doctor Who"). I struggled to connect with him, as did most of the teenage population in Lincoln, Arkansas. I remember telling my friends that my brother had a rare disease that made him behave badly, but since my dad was a teacher, he had connections and kept him in the general high school population.

Arkansas summers are hot and humid. Because I was the only girl in my family, I got the advantage of being the truck driver during hay season. The hay bales we hauled for our cows were all square bales. Round bale equipment didn't arrive at my house until the mid-1980s. Until then, I drove a giant truck and three boys would stack square bales on the back.

Our truck had no air conditioning, or heat for that matter. I kept both windows open in hope of catching just a hint of an occasional breeze. The heat was almost unbearable. I would be covered in sweat in minutes. To make matters worse, slivers of the freshly cut hay would stick to my sweaty skin and clothes. I was always so covered that my mom wouldn't let me sit down on the furniture when I went into the house for a break. I was too gross for my own mother.

It was indeed unglamorous. I was the only girl at my prom with a farmer's tan. When I got frustrated at my obvious skin discoloration earned during those long hours working on the farm, my dad reminded me, "Be proud of where you come from. If you aren't, nobody else will be."

Farm life was tough, yet at the same time enjoyable, and my family worked together. I probably wouldn't have changed it, but I spent many hours of my younger years wondering how the other half lived.

Some of the most fun I had was doing crazy things with friends. They didn't usually live or work on a farm. That fact alone made some of our experiences entertaining.

Here's a little secret. We farm folk have our own way of communicating. A farmer's code, with terms and phrases like fair-to-middling, let me tell you how the cow ate the cabbage, Lord willing and the creek don't rise, come-to-Jesus meeting, one too many roosters in the hen house, once an egg-sucking dog always an egg-sucking dog, and more. We might even be guilty of leading the discussion about the intellectually challenged with the phrase "bless their hearts." If you are from the South, you most likely realize that that phrase is not a statement of empathy.

For instance, when one of our hired hands shut a gate after we pulled the truck through, he shut it with him on the opposite side. Faced with this object between himself and his transportation, he decided to climb over the gate. This was a cardinal sin! You never crawl over a gate because it put stress on the hinges. Dad sat in the truck watching this comedy unfold in the side-view mirror and shaking his head. He muttered under his breath, "Bless his heart." Translated: *That boy is as dumb as nails.* I knew if we ever experienced a zombie apocalypse, that kid was going to be one of the first to go.

I can say the willingness to get dirty has always defined us as a nation, and it's a hallmark of hard work and a hallmark of fun, and dirt is not the enemy.

– Mike Rowe

Chapter 3

Confessions of a Hayseed: Admit Your Mistakes

I had two cousins who would come to visit us from St. Louis. City slickers. They were weird and seemed like easy targets. David was only a few months older than me. Jeffery was the oldest of the cousins by a few years.

The novelty of the farm wore off quickly for David and Jeffery. After that, we had to create our own fun. Just a side note about my cousins: they thought it would be fun to feed calves. Bless their hearts.

One spring afternoon when I was about twelve years old, David and I decided to take the riding lawn mower out for a joy ride. Yep. That's what two tweenagers do on a farm to have fun. Two hundred acres, limited television channels, and our video games consisted of a 1980s Atari gaming system; so clearly the best form of amusement is to pimp the lawn mower and race against time.

This mower was far from the sophisticated John Deere mowers we see today. It was mostly a Case mower. Knowing my dad, it had a Case shell but probably ran with a mutated engine Dad had assembled from many previous mowers. That was how my dad rolled.

There was only one seat, so David and I scrunched on it with one cheek on each side. I had the brake side and steered the rusty machine. David had the clutch and held on to the back of the seat for stability.

David had never hot rodded a lawn mower before. What do people do in St. Louis? Clearly this is prime entertainment.

We raised the deck and kicked that mower into the highest gear. In fact, after a few minutes, I quit slowing down for corners. We were living on the edge. There were a few hills in the yard so I tried my best to get some good air under the mower deck as we flew every bit of three-and-a-half inches off the ground.

We laughed as we made a race course out of my parent's back yard. I decided to take a shortcut next to our old cement cellar. We never used it, because we were convinced it was infested with snakes.

We had a treehouse in our back yard that Dad had built almost seven years earlier. I turned a sharp corner by the treehouse and BAM! With all twenty horses that powered that old riding mower, I slammed into one of the treehouse's wooden pillars.

The impact knocked me off the mower, and I slammed to the ground. I must have been stunned as I looked around in slow motion. I didn't see David. Did the mower roll over him? Did he see the crash coming and abandon the contraption before impact?

I heard some moaning. I looked over at the big oak tree on the other side of the mower. The moaning

continued so I scrambled over the mower. There
I found David sitting up, holding his head. The
collision had thrown him into the tree.

Oh no! Had I nearly killed David? Did he have
permanent brain damage? He appeared to be well,
just dazed. We both looked at the crumpled hood
of the mower and the splintered pillar of the tree
house. The once-majestic stoop that I had played on
for hours a day, hiding from my brother, was now
cattywampus. I feared the whole landing would fall
at any second.

David and I both wanted to laugh, but the sight of
the destruction we caused put fear into us. What
would we tell my parents? We walked slowly to the
house, preparing our speeches along the way. David
quickly reminded me that I was steering. I tried
to push some of the blame onto him as he had the
clutch, not that it would have made any difference.

My mother was busy working in the kitchen. We
had such a strange kitchen. They built the house in
the mid-1970s. Our kitchen had sunflower yellow
walls, orange Formica kitchen counters, royal blue

kitchen carpet and that mustard-yellow refrigerator. Although I like bright colors, our kitchen made a credible case against putting them all in the same room at the same time.

Mom saw our faces and knew we had done something wrong. I blurted out my apology and explanation quickly. I figured that if I spoke really fast, maybe the confession would be better received. She shook her head and leaned over to the window to get a peek at our mess.

I was contemplating our impending punishment. Would Mom make me pay for the repairs? Would she ground me? Would she make David and me take a defensive driving class?

Then the dreaded words came out of her mouth to both of us: "Go tell your father." Oh, man! This was a fate worse than death. Dad was a gentle man, but the thought of disappointing him devastated me. I was okay if he tanned my hide, but to disappoint him…ugh.

As David and I walked to the milk barn, I told him to let me do this alone. I can remember my voice shaking as I said, "This is my responsibility, and you shouldn't have to face this." It was like I said the words but didn't really support what I was saying. To David's credit, he continued to offer to go with me, but I refused.

I walked down the cement steps into the pit of the barn. My dad smiled big at me as he always did. I stood on the bottom step wringing my hands. I knew I had to tell him that I'd destroyed his mower no matter how much I didn't want to.

Again, I blurted out the explanation. This time it was mixed with blubbery tears. He sat on a bucket patiently waiting for me to get control of my emotions. He looked me straight in the eyes and reminded me that I damaged property that he was going to have to fix. He explained that I would have to help him with the repairs. I nodded in agreement. Of course, there was no way I was going to disagree with him.

Then the most remarkable thing happened. He got up, hugged me, and thanked me for taking responsibility and admitting my mistake. He said,

"The difference between good people and bad people is that good people will admit what they have done. Bad people will hide their mistakes."

Okay, so maybe this was the beginning of my crime streak. But at least I was an honest criminal!

Not all of my adventures were as much fun. On one Memorial Day weekend, my city slicker cousins came for another visit. My grandparents had a farm that was much larger than my parents' farm. It was 500 acres. However, I knew every inch of that farm because I lived so close to them. I was the unofficial tour guide when my cousins decided they wanted to go exploring. When they were ready to go, I packed my cousins up into the old farm truck and headed up the mountain.

Let's talk a little about learning to drive on the farm. There is no motor vehicle law governing the farm. I started driving the hated hay truck when I was about ten years old. My older brother probably started driving it even younger. If you could see over the dash, you were ready to start driving.

The true test of learning to drive on the farm at such a young age is whether you were able to push the clutch all the way in, change gears, and avoid running off the mountain—all at the same time. Most boys I knew when I was growing up were able to navigate trucks and gooseneck trailers by the time they were fourteen. They just weren't legally allowed on the road for another year, which is not to say it didn't happen. Most officers knew every kid who was driving and would look the other way if it involved the farm. Regardless, all of us were driving by the age of fifteen.

The trucks we drove on the farm were in serious need of repair, and I'm not talking a few scratches. My favorite truck was an early-1970s model four-wheel-drive Chevy. It had lost its driver's side door somewhere along the way. That feature made it a sport vehicle for us.

When I fed hay to the cows in the evening after their last milking, I would put the truck in gear and aim it for the gate. As I came close to it, I would then get out and run to the gate. I'd open it and let the truck drive itself through. Once the truck was clear of the gate, I would latch it (from the correct side, I might add), race to the truck, and jump in. I referred to it as efficiency. Even at a young age, I was looking for ways to improve efficiency.

But now back to exploring.

My cousins and I parked at the edge of the largest hay field. It sat between two very large hills and was close to one hundred acres. It was well into summer, and the Bermuda was thick and ready for the cutting. The breeze blew the tall grass in soft waves. Even though the grass was beautiful—almost breathtaking—I knew we were just weeks away from the dreaded hay hauling again.

Ugh. I shrugged it off and guided my cousins to the creek. We had good fishing in the Barren Fork Creek. I never knew why it was called Barren Fork, but I knew it was the creek. And no, we did not say "crick." I may have been raised in the great hog nation of Arkansas, but I was taught to speak.

We came to the little clearing in the brushy undergrowth that signaled my favorite fishing spot.

I carefully watched the ground beneath my steps. The area close to the creek would sometimes house large water moccasins. These snakes hated people. Water moccasins will chase you just for sport. The old saying that they are more scared of you than you are of them is a complete misunderstanding of these creatures.

I was almost through the underbrush when my cousin Jeff shouted, "Look!" He was pointing to the creek edge just upriver—or I guess *upcreek* in this case. There sat an old white flat-bottom boat. Of course, this needed to be investigated. Our step increased. We started carelessly treading forward as we were focused on our new find.

We waded into the water to reach the boat. It was abandoned. The white paint was splintering off. The wood had started warping in the rear, leaving a large bowed-out section. Jeff climbed in first. David quickly followed. What do tweenagers do when they find an abandoned boat? They sink it.

David ripped the seat from the boat and tossed it overboard. Jeff started jabbing the looser boards with a large stick, trying to pry them apart. My brother helped him while I stood look out. David, being the only person smart enough to carry a hatchet, started chopping the bottom. Water started to percolate through the holes.

It was exhausting work sinking a boat. We left the boat to finish sinking to the bottom of the creek and headed for more land to explore.

That evening at my grandmother's table, we all enjoyed her amazing cooking. We were laughing at one another's jokes and listening to my cousins tell stories of city life when we heard a loud rap at the door.

My grandfather answered the door. There stood a large, bearded man I had never seen before. He wore a Dickies-brand pair of overalls with rubber boots. He asked Grandpa if he had seen anyone on the creek in the last few weeks. Grandpa, a bit confused, said no, but that he didn't make it a point to walk over there often.

Well, it seems that someone had sunk this man's boat. I gasped. My eyes were wide. My heart was beating. The realization was kicking in on my cousins as well. The boat wasn't abandoned after all. Oh, no! We were all guilty of sinking this man's boat. Jeff, David, and my brother all sat with their mouths drooping. I think Jeff was even wheezing a little as he often did when he got nervous.

As Grandpa finished his discussion and returned to the table, all of our eyes dropped to our plates. Grandpa was shaking his head telling Grandma that he couldn't believe people. They even went so far as to brainstorm on possible offenders, not realizing the criminals sat in front of them.

My sweet little four-foot-nine grandmother finally declared a neighbor boy as clearly being the perpetrator. In her sweet, gentle voice, she said, "Once an egg-sucking dog, always an egg-sucking dog."

At that moment, the scene from Jesus' last supper popped into my head. At least my supper was amazing. It was everything you think of when you think of Southern food—fried chicken, mashed potatoes, home-grown cow peas, and chocolate chip cookies for dessert.

Needless to say, the rest of our meal was quiet and lost any taste. Later that night, my cousins, brother, and I agreed to never speak of the boat incident again.

But I couldn't get the boat incident out of my mind. Dad was a major influence in my life, as well as the life of many people in my community. Admitting mistakes, communicating in a way people understood and being proud of who you are, were qualities of greatness in his mind.

Here was the lingering thought I had: would Dad want me to admit this mistake? Deep inside, I knew the answer. I couldn't speak for the others involved in the boat incident, but I could do the right thing.

It took a while to get up the courage to tell Dad. It would not be until our adult years that we spoke of the vandalism to an aquatic vehicle again. And yes, when Dad finally found out about it, he grounded me.

Always do right. This will gratify some people and astonish the rest.

– Mark Twain

Chapter 4

Communicate Until the Cows Come Home

Growing up on a farm was hard. The only entertainment I could muster was fishing, playing with my 4-H projects, watching reruns of *Gilligan's Island*, and hiking.

I loved hiking most of all. We had relatively easy terrain on the farm. There were no major hills, but we had many boulders I could perch on like an Indian scout.

I took my Suffolk lamb, Zorro, on several of my hiking adventures. Yes, this is not a lie. My best friend and trusty sidekick at one time was a sheep! Dad bought him for me as an experiment for a 4-H project. If I could raise him and learn to show him, maybe we would get into lamb shows.

Dad was a vocational agriculture (vo-ag) teacher. He loved agriculture. I mean he loved everything about it. Not only did he milk cows twice a day, he also taught a classroom full of eager students the fundamentals of production agriculture. In fact, the only way I could get his attention during the school day was to address him as "Mr. Webb."

Learning to raise a new animal was fun for him, and being that he was a bit competitive, showing that animal was icing on the cake.

Zorro was really young when I first got him. He was scared of everything. I spent hours in his pen just sitting on the ground talking to him, in the hope he would decide I was friendly.

My efforts paid off. He quickly figured out that I was the person who controlled his food. Food he liked. He liked it a lot. Even though Zorro's pen was nowhere near our house, he could hear our sliding glass door open and he would start bleating. There was no doubt that his "Baaah!" meant "Bring me more food!"

Lamb show judges look for powerful back legs. To build up Zorro's leg muscles, Dad built a steep staircase on his gate. Zorro would stand with his front legs braced on those stairs so his head could peek over the gate. Constant standing in that position strengthened Zorro's back legs.

I decided one day to take him for a walk. He walked next to me like a dog on a leash. The next day, I did the same.

Then I got brave. I flipped the leash over his back and called him. He came to me. He knew his name! What sheep knows his name? From that point on, I never haltered Zorro. I simply let him out of his pen, and we would go hiking. He would run, jump, and do flips. He eventually figured out how to read my hand signals and would flip by command.

For the Fourth of July, Zorro and I were the entertainment. I brought him down from the pen and performed an impromptu show of Zorro flips and stops.

Zorro was a hit. Laughter was as thick as the fireworks smoke.

When the party was over, Dad put his arm around my shoulder and said, "When you learn to communicate with each other, the fun begins!" Of course, he was chuckling and his eyes were filled with glee. Or maybe that was tears of joy that his daughter had become a lamb whisperer.

During high school, I was active in Future Farmers of America (FFA). Today this is simply referenced as FFA. But I'm from the old school and still reference it as Future Farmers of America. Because Dad, (Mr. Webb) was the vo-ag teacher, by default that made him the FFA advisor as well. It was a role he embraced with every cell of his being.

He had a competitive nature. He sought out contests, and he intended to dominate each one. He was a quiet man, but he had a great sense of humor. For him to chase winning with such voracity was really a joy to watch and be part of. Being the daughter of a vo-ag teacher is exciting and challenging. I had the distinct pleasure of being part of almost every contest as well.

Living on a dairy farm naturally connected us to dairy cattle shows. We worked for months breaking calves to lead, conditioning them and fitting them for show. Each calf had its own unique personality.

It's truly amazing how much strength a little Guernsey calf can muster. I was dragged through our dry lot by feisty calves more times than I care to remember.

Since we showed in summer and fall, it always seemed to be sizzling hot outside. Every day, twice a day, I haltered up those calves and attempted to train them to show. I wanted them to become familiar with my touch, learn to walk with grace and ease, and be gentle in their stance. I was in training too. In a show, the difference between the ring of champions, referred to as purple circle, and second place is the person on the halter.

All that work would eventually pay off in the ring. Dad knew how to condition the animals; so when we walked in the ring with our calves, the officials noticed. We were trained to get the officials' attention and position the calves in the most strategic position. We also learned to quickly size up competition. We were blessed having a great coach for a dad. It also didn't hurt to have good dairy genetics and a tradition for dairy excellence on our side. We seldom left a show upset.

With all that said, the true sportsman of my dad came through. If a young exhibitor struggled fitting their animal, Dad was the first to lend a hand. If someone needed supplies or equipment, they knew they could count on him. Exhibitors sought his advice as long as I can remember. He was giving, respectful, and genuinely happy to help. He was the respected leader every time he walked into a show barn.

One day, a stranger approached me in the show barn. He said he was interested in buying my calf. I ran into this conversation often. People always wanted to buy Dad's stock, but he seldom sold any.

I told the gentleman that none of our calves were for sale. He said, "I brought $500 like the sign said." I know I understood the words coming out of his mouth, but they didn't make any sense. Puzzled, I asked, "Sign? What sign?" He pointed to the tie area where our show string stood.

There above my calf—the winning calf, by the way—was a sign fashioned out of cardboard that read, "For Sale: Registered Guernsey, $500" followed by our phone number. What makes that funny is that a calf of that quality would generally sell for $3,000.

Recognizing that someone was pranking us, I quickly took the sign down, but the phone calls my mom received didn't end for days. I showed Dad the sign, and he chuckled with all 190 pounds of him. "Hummel, that fiend." A neighboring vo-ag teacher was responsible for this prank.

Dad laughed and started plotting his counterattack. He loved joking around. "Always appreciate a good joke, and laugh at yourself," he said. "Let's see what Hummel says next week after I put an ad in the paper selling his mule."

If you always do what interests you, at least one person is pleased.

– Katharine Hepburn

 **CHAPTER 5**

Leaders Serve Others

When I left the farm for college, I learned about the concept of servant-leadership. Most people have a weird notion that leaders are to be served by their followers. This servant-leadership concept seems to mystify people. It has always confused me, too.

Why is that concept so mysterious and hard to define? And then why is it so hard for others to live?

Servant-leadership is the act of serving others you lead by placing their needs before your own. The role of leader is often designated by title or responsibility in an organization. However, it isn't unusual for a person without a title or leadership role to be considered as a leader among his or her peers. When you drill down to why people consider someone a leader, you'll find the individual possesses a set of leadership traits. Most likely, you'll find servant-leadership to be one of them.

I was blessed that I got to see servant-leadership lived out in its truest and simplest form. Dad was probably the closest thing to a veterinarian in our neck of the woods. Neighbors knew they could call him when they needed help with their animals.

Since we had a dairy, we nearly always had good colostrum—the first milk after a cow gives birth—available. It's one of the best foods for ailing newborn calves. Many neighbors were in need of this remedy.

Dad would roll out of bed at 5:00 a.m. to milk cows, clean the barn, and then teach school all day. After he returned home in the afternoon, he'd milk cows again, feed cattle, and then finally drag a very worn-out body to bed. Yet if a neighbor needed him to look at an animal, no matter how tired he was, he would somehow fit it into his day.

Milk fever is a dangerous disease that attacks dairy cattle without warning. I can remember getting milk from the barn to start my chore of feeding those ferocious calves, when Mom asked Dad to take a call in the barn (yes, we had a phone in the milk room).

It was our neighbor, Bill. Dad exchanged a few words with him and almost ran over me dashing to get to his little tackle box of vet supplies. He asked me to finish the cows in the barn and assured me that he would be back. Bill's Jersey was down. They knew it was milk fever. Dad also knew this cow was a quality animal with tremendous genetic potential. Most importantly though, it was Bill's little girl's beloved pet.

Once he arrived, Dad had to pump calcium into the cow as quickly as he could, because she was nearly gone. And yes, he saved the day.

Dad never got to save the day when it was convenient timing. And he never asked to be paid. Above that, he didn't expect payment and would have been insulted if someone had offered.

How do I know he led a servant life? Every Christmas, we experienced one of the greatest sights. Our neighbors, nearly every single one, delivered homemade goodies to our front door. I thought at the time that it was something everyone did. But as I matured I realized that our neighbors saw it as their opportunity to say thanks to someone who was there in crises and good times.

Dad would always say, "Serving others is a blessing. Why would you not share in blessings? Seeking unselfish greater good for others is rewarding."

Here's another example of Dad practicing servant leadership. Sometimes that greater good can actually hurt.

I know this probably seems strange to most people, but showing cattle was our family's hobby. Agriculture is so much more than cows, plows, chicks, and hicks. There is tremendous technology and science involved in modern agriculture.

Even when I was young, the impact of science was great. Cows were artificially inseminated so as to eliminate the need and danger of raising a dairy bull. And nutrition was a key element to ensuring a healthy diet for our cows. The trace minerals were measured to the nth degree. Therefore, opportunities to show off the beauty of an animal that housed all the right genetics and displayed the characteristics we sought as dairy farmers, were priceless moments.

Oh, the stories from the show barns I could tell. There were highly competitive moments. There were buckets thrown out of anger. There were frustrations with misbehaving cattle. There was the revelation that our genetics were not the best in show. But there were also moments of kindness, brotherhood, fellowship, sportsmanship—and yes, servant leadership.

The Ozark Empire Fair in Springfield, Missouri was one of our favorite shows, mainly because it was close. It was 1982. That year I had a ringer. This calf grew from the moment she landed on earth and seemed to never stop. She stood at least six inches taller than any other calf in her previous competition. I think some breeders questioned her date of birth, but with Dad's reputation for integrity, people immediately shook that thought off.

The day of the show was frantic. It started at 4:00 a.m. with washing our cattle, cleaning the bedding, and grooming each one for their appearance in the ring.

About an hour before the show started, a young man approached my dad. We knew who he was. We had scouted the barns earlier that week. He was my competition. He had a stellar calf in the same class as my calf, Tonya.

Here he stood before my dad with a set of clippers that had died half way through grooming his heifer. My heart skipped a beat. His calf looked like it had the mange. Yay! My calf will easily win the class, and then we will once again parade through the purple circle.

So what did my dad do? Not only did he loan the young man his favorite clippers, he actually touched up some areas the kid had missed. (Gasp!) He was going beyond being helpful. He was working for the enemy!

I asked him why he did that. He once again spoke wisdom. He told me not to fear good competition.

He assured me that is would make me better.

And better I had to be. I worked that calf in that arena, positioned her, and kept the eye of the judge on her as much as possible. I knew she was a tad taller than my competitor's calf, so I instinctively lined up Tonya's massive body as close as I could to his calf.

But to no avail. Tonya received a second place ribbon that day. His calf not only won the class, but won the show.

I felt bad until Dad returned to the barn with a grin on his face. He grabbed my shoulders and said, "I'm proud of you, CC." CC was my nickname. "Tonya wasn't the best today, but you were." He explained that he watched the judge and knew he struggled with the decision. He knew there was competition, and I was clearly working hard. All those things were noticed. Yes, my calf lost, but my abilities improved because of the challenge provided by someone else's good efforts.

That young man returned to that show for years and struck up a friendship with my dad. He always thanked him for his best cattle show experience. And I enjoyed every minute of it! Oh, out of all my ribbons I've kept over the years, that's the only red ribbon that remains.

Success is a lousy teacher. It seduces smart people into thinking they can't lose.

– Bill Gates

 **CHAPTER 6**

Live with Passion and Purpose

As I entered the work world, I felt it was important to find my purpose. So I reflected on the twin passions of my father: farming and teaching.

My Dad, Dwayne Webb, was a vocational agriculture teacher and the advisor to the local chapter of the Future Farmers of America (FFA). Probably the largest youth organization in the United States, the FFA has 610,240 members and 7,665 chapters in U.S. high schools. The mission of the FFA is to promote agriculture education and provide skills to help students mature and develop employable skill sets.

It is estimated that one American farmer feeds 155 people. That number is growing every day, which is great news, since, as of today, 805 million people in the world are food-insecure. Innovation and science will be critical to the successful mission to feed an ever-growing population.

Regardless of your opinions of modern agriculture, you have to recognize the sustained efforts of individuals to live their passions. Marathon runners, who prepare twelve months for one race, will train more than 10,000 hours to reach their peak. Basketball great Kobe Bryant practiced well over 10,000 hours in his career. The Beatles performed live in Hamburg, Germany over 1,200 times from 1960 to 1964, amassing more than 10,000 hours of playing time.

My Dad spent three hours each morning and four hours each evening farming. Plus, he dedicated eight hours a day to educating youth in how to establish a work ethic and love agriculture. By my calculations, he worked fifteen hours a day, every day. Each day he taught, his students performed better. He was a lifelong learner, applying new methods to teaching. He sought new and improved agricultural methods which he needed to stay marginally profitable and feed those 155 people. In my estimation, he spent well over 200,000 hours living his twin passions.

Remember that passion leads through the pain; passion gives you energy. He found it. I sought it. We all need to live it.

In the end, it's not the years in your life that count. It's the life in your years.

– Abraham Lincoln

 **CHAPTER 7**

How to be Influential without Getting Shot

Now back to my gateway crimes. Knowing what I knew from growing up, how did I end up being the center of a crime scene?

More backstory:

My tale begins a few months earlier on the first day of my new job. The box of items I brought for my office was much heavier on one end, which made carrying it awkward. I had stuffed it full of family photos, airplane books (those that you can read on one leg of a trip), and new pens—red, blue, purple, and green. I stumbled through the hallway hoping someone would offer to help. No such luck.

Everyone avoided eye contact, which seemed a little too obvious to me.

Never mind. I was excited about the possibilities of this new job. Though it wasn't in the type of industry I had hoped for, this company offered a promotion, more money, more responsibility, and more challenges—all truly motivating factors for me.

Despite those degrees in agriculture, I never saw myself farming full time, even though my husband and I live on a small farm. I dreamed of climbing the corporate ladder. Early in my career, I envisioned myself as an influencer—at least, an aspiring influencer.

But my first real opportunity to influence others in the corporate arena came when I was hired by a poultry company (did you think chicken just magically appears in the supermarket?) as its first director of talent development. That title sounded good as I introduced myself to my officemates. When asked what I was going to do, I simply explained that my job was to inspire.

I was determined to succeed in this new position. I had spent several days researching how to influence people prior to moving into my new role. I wanted to make an impact on my new team and the company as a whole. I saw my new role as something more than simply providing compliance training. It would provide options and future opportunity for advancement for people who felt they had none.

Many of the self-help books refer to influence in theoretical studies. Find the right behavior and use personal motivation factors and personal ability theories…yada, yada, yada. No doubt if you had a PhD, this would all guarantee an incredible impact. But for me, the plan to influence others was so much simpler.

This is the model that I was going to use.

> *Influence = Strength + Intelligence*
> *+ Go-to Person + Communication Skills*

I was convinced that this was the way to do it—be the person of influence and eventually build my own department that would impact the company. I would show people how strong and assertive I could be. I would show the company the depths of my intellect and abilities. I would be that person that others call on to make things happen because of my total commitment to the cause. And in the process, I would obviously wow everyone with my grace and uncanny ability to communicate with others, regardless of their positions in the company hierarchy.

This should be simple and achievable. Just stick to the plan.

My first days were spent getting to know the people. They were a good mix of people. Some people were very friendly and we bonded very quickly. Others were clearly very strategic. Then, of course, there were those I quickly learned to keep a safe distance from, as they tended to gossip.

Because of my commitment to the plan, my role flourished. I easily worked my way into department meetings and became a valued resource—at least in my mind. I was especially devoted to making certain the senior staff saw me as an integral resource who was key to achieving company goals.

I scheduled a meeting one morning before the crack of dawn just so I could meet with the full executive team before facilitating a communications study. I had studied their communication styles, prepared handouts according to their needs, easily presented my case, and won their buy-in.

Phew! The hard stuff for the day was over. Now I could move on to the communication study.

I held my class in the local community room next to the new bank in town. Training space in a small town is always a bit tricky. The really good spaces would have standing reservations with the local civic groups like Masons, Kiwanis, Rotary, and Little League.

I planned carefully so I could reserve this newest, nicest meeting space in town. I wanted to make certain the environment was comfortable and inviting. Employees often regard training as an inconvenience that interferes with their workload. It was important to me that the teams feel appreciated and valued so they would want to come to these classes.

I was training the accounting team that day. It was a small team, but it was one that could certainly use some understanding of the intricate details of communication styles. They had a leader named Mike who was anxious to build rapport and inspire his team.

Mike was a forty-something guy who was new to the company. Frankly, Mike was new to the industry. He certainly knew how to handle a calculator, but he was lost in the poultry industry.

He was that guy who walks through the hall with his head held low—not because of a lack of confidence, but because he is always thinking. Mike was a man on a mission. He already recognized that his team didn't embrace his leadership. To be fair, he had only been on the job for two months, and it takes time to build rapport. I planned a communication exercise. It was a great first step. This should be easy.

The team truly only had two modes of communication: e-mail and texting. This was a team that shouldn't struggle at all. There was likely another underlying issue causing the team to be slow to gel. My activity would help the team members identify each person's communication preferences. It was always a good exercise.

To be effective and win, it is vital to communicate in a manner that the receiver can associate with and understand. This is the cause of so many misunderstandings in the world. We focus too much on our own communication preferences instead of adapting to the communication preferences and needs of the audience.

The class was great. The team members were engaged, expressing themselves, and taking notes. You couldn't ask for a better, more teachable group. Now was the time to unveil the last game. It would allow them to take what they had learned and apply it in a fun way to achieve an objective.

I made three circles on the floor with rope. I then divided the team and put three people in each circle.

The people in the first circle were given a diagram to recreate. However, they could not speak to the other team members, nor leave their circle.

The people in the second circle were given no instructions except they also couldn't leave their circle.

The people in the third circle were blindfolded and told not to leave their circle. I scattered toys throughout their circle once they were blindfolded.

This game had been successful so many times before. Nothing could possibly go wrong.

After about ten minutes, the first two groups of people were starting to figure out a method of communication that would work. They used a primitive form of sign language.

At that moment, two uniformed police officers walk through the back door. The communication efforts ceased as all of everyone's attention was drawn to the officers—except, of course, for the blindfolded jokers crawling all over the floor feeling for more toys.

I quickly moved over to the officers and asked if there was a problem. I knew the team was having a good time and was getting a little rowdy with laughter. Surely the people at the bank didn't call the cops on us.

The more senior officer explained that a silent alarm went off in the bank next door. They had just finished working with the bank to identify the source of the alarm. It was a faulty night teller machine.

However, as part of their protocol, they have to check out the surrounding area. He asked me to explain what was going on. I explained the communication training activities and noted this was their final game. Slowly a smile appeared on the officer's face. He joked that he knew someone in the class. The officers quickly exited the same way they came in, and class resumed.

Another ten to fifteen minutes escaped as the accounting team worked on their objective. Finally, they finished. What a challenge for them. Relieved, I started clapping, stood up, and asked the blindfolded people to remove their blindfold and look at what they had built with their toys.

At that moment I looked at the front door. Standing on the outside of the large industrial-sized glass door was a man dressed in street clothes with a gun drawn by his side. On his gun holster was a police badge. He pointed at the team member nearest the door and yelled, "Get down! Get down!"

Shocked and slightly terrified, I turned quickly to get down. A million thoughts are racing through my mind. I'm the director of talent management. I'm in charge of this activity. I should have a plan for something like this.

As I squatted there collecting my thoughts, I realized what the policeman was looking at. He saw three people sitting on the floor blindfolded—in a room next to a bank where a silent alarm had just gone off.

I scurried over to the door to talk with him. With the help of the police officers who visited the class earlier, I was able to explain the situation and appease the plainclothes police officer.

It was quite an ordeal. The police department had moved quickly to handle our "hostage" situation. Outside our window were dozens of police cars staged with lights and sirens off. I overheard one of the officers cancel the SWAT team—*the SWAT team*!

I returned to work after lunch. I was exhausted. It's not every day I get held at gun point by a police officer. I settled in behind my desk to check my e-mail.

I heard a voice in my doorway, "We need to talk about training." I looked up. There stood the president of the company with a bandana draped across his nose and mouth to imitate a burglar. He busted out in a bold chuckle that echoed down the hall.

Sigh. So much for influence. He was the same person I had worked so hard to influence earlier that morning. I was convinced that the efforts to show strength and intelligence from this morning were lost in the wake of the whole storm surrounding the "hostage" incident.

The next few weeks were insufferable. Eventually I (mostly) lived down the humiliation of nearly getting nine members of my company's accounting team shot. I was starting to focus again.

I decided I needed some retail therapy. A few new clothes would pick up my spirits. It worked like a charm. I was ready to take on the world again.

The next day I put on one of my new outfits and went to work early with high hopes of tackling the pile of administrative chores on my desk. I walked through the almost empty hallway and stopped to chat with James, one of our vice presidents.

James is that executive who never fit the mold. He is a larger-than-life fellow who explodes with energy everywhere he goes. I always chuckled when he tried to whisper a secret with his big bold voice. That whisper could clearly be heard seven offices down, but he was certain he had just had a confidential conversation.

James had been my champion in coming to the company, so I always felt somewhat connected to him.

As I turned to leave, James stopped me. He said, "I'm only doing this because I am your friend." He then proceeded to pull the gigantic size ten sticker off the back of my new pants.

Thank God for James being observant and brave enough to help me with my wardrobe malfunction. But I felt like such a goober. How was I supposed to prove I was an influential member of the management team if I couldn't pull the sticker off of the new pants? I could feel my ability to influence pulling away from me.

Those first few weeks resembled little of the ideal picture of my influence as a leader in my new company. Looking back, it was a great lesson in flexibility and humility—two traits that I improved through those hard moments. I probably learned more than what I taught others those few weeks— more about myself and more about influencing and leadership. And we made a few great memories in the process. That might be the most important outcome of all.

But this didn't seem to fit my influence model. This felt different. Maybe my original model needed tweaking. Clearly to be influential I needed to be able to *communicate* in such a way to save the lives of my participants in training, and *communicate* my appreciation to James for saving me from being embarrassed. Seems like one of those good lessons from Dad.

I'm not funny. What I am is brave.

– Lucille Ball

CHAPTER 8

Being Influential Should Not Be a Crime

Even though the first few weeks of my new job at the poultry company didn't go quite as planned, I still wanted to make an impression. Maybe being an influencer based on my knowledge and intellect wasn't in the cards. "I know," I thought, "I'll work on the Go-to Person philosophy. I can make things happen. That will make me an influential person."

I formulated my plan. I decided to stay thirty minutes late every day. I had considered coming in to work thirty minutes early, but let's face it, that was REALLY hard work. I had also decided to volunteer for every project where I could offer any value. I was even willing to go so far as to laugh at every ridiculous joke that non-funny people said.

During one of the program presentations, I brought in some of our out-of-town team members. I helped them set up a Wow! kind of presentation for the senior staff. Everyone seemed impressed. "Great!" I thought, "Another victory."

The presenters quickly disbanded and prepared to head back to their locations. They left word for me that they would need a ride to the airport the following morning. Their flight was at six o'clock a.m. "Six a.m.? Who catches a flight at that hour?"

The airline required them to check in at the airport an hour before their flight. I quickly realized that in order to deliver them to the airport at 5:00, I would have to leave my house around 3:45 a.m. That meant getting up no later than 3:00.

Okay, now again, I was focused on achieving the influential status of go-to person. A proper go-to person doesn't complain, and you can always count on her.

After some thought, I realized that this person sleeps past 3:00 a.m. It was clear that I was going to have to work smarter, not harder, if I was going to be a go-to person.

I coordinated with the team to check out a company van and leave it at the airport. I arranged for a coworker to drop me off at 8:00 a.m. to pick it up. I instructed them to park in short-term parking and leave the keys under the floor mat. Ah ha. That's thinking!

The next morning at 8:00 a.m., my coworker takes me to the short-term parking lot and we locate a white van. I open the door of the unlocked van, and locate the keys under the floor mat. I jump in and start the van and wave to my coworker as she drives away.

As I headed back to the office, I thought proudly to myself, "I am definitely an asset to this company. I am willing to help everyone and no job is beneath me. This will make me more influential to everyone in the company."

As soon as I returned to the office, I was met by a coworker, Kurt, asking for keys to the van. He needed it and had already okayed it through the company van coordinator, Ms. Dawn. I lovingly called her The Auto Nazi. I gave him the keys and hurried off to my office to influence more people.

There are a few things you need to know about Ms. Dawn. She is stern and set in her ways. She is a person who has memorized the organization chart and found it comfortable to work in silos. There is no gray area with Ms. Dawn. On top of all of that, she is a Yankee living in the rural South. But she is an amazing asset to the company with her incredible attention to detail and task-management mad skills.

I was still learning my way at my new company, but one fact I learned quickly was that you never, ever crossed Ms. Dawn.

I heard a knock on my door jam. I look up to see the unforgiving face of Ms. Dawn. She asks where the van is. My heart sank. Dang that Kurt, I knew I couldn't trust him. He told me he had okayed it, but clearly he hadn't. I told Ms. Dawn, "Kurt has it."

"No...where is *our* van?" Ms. Dawn responded, "This is *not* our van." She dangles the keys at me, shaking them as if to say, "You moron! You picked up the wrong van!"

I could feel the blood draining from my face. I gasped. My ears began to tingle, and the lights started to dim. I realized the severity of the issue.

"Clearly there were two white vans in short-term parking. I picked up one and another company picked up the other," I explained. "I'll just find the owner of the other van and fix this."

I hurried to the van, rummaged through the glove box frantically attempting to locate an owner's name. Yes! I found the insurance card! Unfortunately, the owner was a company, not a person.

I pulled out my cell phone and called the insurance company in hopes of finding a nice young person who would disregard the rules and give me the pertinent information I needed. No such luck.

The voice on the other end of the line clearly belonged to a lady closer to retirement than me.

I told her my story of two vans left unlocked in a parking lot with the keys inside—not a scenario anyone feels proud to explain to an insurance company representative. I explained that her client and I had mistakenly taken each other's vans. Now I would like ours back.

The customer service representative listened patiently. She then asked for me to repeat the story.

There was a long pause. Then I heard this sound that reminded me of sandpaper hitting a rough plane of wood. I quickly figured out that the representative was snickering uncontrollably.

"Well," the representative responded, "This is the most interesting story I have heard in the forty years I have worked in the insurance industry. I will be happy to give you a phone number that you can try."

Whew! I jotted down the phone number. I saw a light at the end of the tunnel.

I dialed the number which rang at the company that owned the other van. Unfortunately, the phone number just rolled to voice mail. "This *can't* be happening," I thought.

By this time, Ms. Dawn had joined me by the side of the van door. She looked pale and troubled. I had to find a solution quick.

"Maybe you should report the van," Ms. Dawn suggested. I pondered what would happen if I followed her advice. What does a person do when they find themselves guilty of grand theft auto? Is this a career-ending move? How influential would I be to the company if I had a rap sheet? Maybe I'd be more influential to the prisoners in the jail where I would undoubtedly spend the next holiday. Ugh!

"You are right," I replied to Ms. Dawn. "Let's make that call."

Actually, inside my head, I was screaming, "*What the heck, are you thinking?*"

As we walked the long, dark corridor to Ms. Dawn's office, I was stopped by one of our coworkers, Sarah. You never really saw Sarah in the office. Nobody actually knew what Sarah did for the company. Even worse, Sarah was that lady whom the office administration had nicknamed Sybil, after the 1976 movie about the woman who suffered from multiple personality syndrome.

I wondered who Sarah was going to be today. Was she going to be a sweet, considerate friend interested in everyone? Or was she going to be the office terrorist, seeking out people to insult and sabotage as she walked through the halls?

Sarah asked, "Did you find the van okay?" What a comment to make! Of course we didn't or I wouldn't be here. The jokes were already starting. I hadn't even been arraigned yet.

"What do you mean?" I replied. Sarah went on to explain that she felt badly for one of the travelers and decided to help them out by giving them a lift to the airport early this morning. She dropped our company's van off behind the dumpster near the back of the company parking lot.

Things were starting to crystallize now. No one had taken our van and it was parked in our parking lot.

However, I had just taken a van that didn't belong to me. (Gasp!)

How could Sarah change the plans and not tell me? The idea of justifiable homicide ran through my mind. I entertained thoughts of hiding Sarah's lifeless body in the van behind the dumpster near the back of the company parking lot. Sarah was small—I had no doubt I could take her.

I snapped back to reality. The situation had now reached a new low. I wasn't sure how I was going to explain this to a police officer. The tingling started again. This time I decided it was time for action.

In my best belle voice I turned to Ms. Dawn and said, "Ms. Dawn, would you be so kind as to pick me up from the airport?"

"Sure," Ms. Dawn responded, "What are you going to do?"

I replied, "What every respectable thief does when caught. I'm going to return the van to the spot I found it, put the keys back under the mat, and run like the devil." Then I smiled, just as Grandma Jessie had taught me.

Upon returning from the airport after depositing the hot van, I entered the building exhausted. You would be amazed at how tiring it is to lead an accidental life of crime.

It didn't take long for the story to get out. I had no sooner returned from the airport and turned the corner to my office when I met a corridor full of people. The building was abuzz with people making every snarky comment they could think of.

I had to tell the story to at least a dozen people. I grumbled to myself, "They really should listen better so I wouldn't have to relive the story all over again." Actually, the jokes they were making were quite funny. In moments, I found myself laughing with them at me.

I somehow found enough energy to finish out the day. I chuckled to myself on my drive back home that evening. What a strange experience it was.

"Oh my," I whispered to myself as I thought of my failed attempt at establishing myself as an influencer and go-to person in my company. I hoped I wouldn't forever be known as the girl who stole the van at the airport. Or the girl who caused the Benton County SWAT team to deploy. But I will say, *laughing at myself,* just like Dad taught me, seemed to have an impact on my ability to build rapport with others. Let's just hope I have fewer opportunities in the future...

Everything is funny, as long as it's happening to somebody else.

– Will Rogers

 **C**HAPTER **9**

Learning from a Redneck on the Golf Course

As with most sophisticated companies, there is always that special day budgeted for and set aside for fellowship and bonding. In the poultry company I worked for, that day comes in the form of a golf tournament.

Golfing is hard for me. I'm not a competent golfer, but I golf for the thrill of learning something new, so I actually looked forward to this day. It's one day—four hours of golfing and two hours of mingling with coworkers who I may not know very well—full of laughing and good-hearted smack talk.

The day of the big golf tournament arrived. On the

drive to the golf course, I was preoccupied by the anticipation of who would be on my team.

In other tournaments with other companies, I had landed on teams with those guys who took the game so seriously that I was terrified I would make a bad swing and get "the look."

You know the look. It's the "why are you even here?" look. It is trademarked by the same guys who beat their clubs on the ground when the ball doesn't cooperate. Clearly it was the club's fault. It deserved to be punished.

At other tournaments, I had drawn the short straw and ended up on a team with three drunks. In a way, that was entertaining, but eventually it became rude and disgusting. Those golfers were the ones that drank everything the cart girl brought by. Then they would strategize. Now that was where the entertainment began.

The drunk golfers would determine the course's length, which direction it would curve, check the wind, stretch, and then stumble to the box.

Sometimes, through the grace of God, they actually hit the ball. When they missed, it was always deemed "a practice swing."

I arrived at the golf course. Enough reminiscing. The moment of truth had come: who would be on my team?

The teams were announced. Phew, I got lucky. I knew two of my teammates—Doug and Steven. Both were good golfers. Maybe this would be the year I would be on a winning team. However, I had not met one team member before—Ralph.

The teams gathered around the carts and it was go time. I joined Doug and Steven as they started assembling their cart. They both had that tattered golfer look. Their worn bags were faded by countless hours of sun, their shoes needed polish, their gloves molded to the curves of their hands.

Then along swaggered Ralph, the final team member. I could spot him miles away. He showed up in cut-off jeans, a button-up plaid western-cut shirt, and a Bud Light ball cap. He hadn't shaved and had that beer gut stressing the buttons on his shirt.

"Perfect," I thought. He was the epitome of the redneck stereotype. A dozen Jeff Foxworthy redneck jokes came to mind ("If you go to a family reunion because you think it would be a good place to meet women, if people stop at your house because they think you are having a yard sale, if you list your parole officer as a reference, then you might be a redneck."). And of course I would get to spend the whole day riding in his cart learning about him, his wife, his ex-wife, the truck on blocks outside of his bedroom window, when the tornado hit the trailer park, and no telling what else. He truly looked like a country music song come to life.

The first hole was good. Steven led the charge with an incredible 250-yard drive right down the fairway. Great positioning. Doug stepped up and put us on the greens. Ralph's ball shanked hard to the right and was lost in the trees. My ball traveled miraculously from the tee to the cart path. At least it was easy to find.

Steven finished off the hole as he putted us in. Par. We're on a streak. At least Doug and Steven are.

Holes two, three, and four were basically the same as the first. Yes, my balls were always easy to locate as they had little to no distance. Ralph's balls were unpredictable and somewhat dangerous.

In the cart, Ralph offered me some advice, "Your stance is wrong. Widen your stance, and don't be afraid to hit the ground." "Okay," I said but I really thought to myself, "What can some redneck tell me about golf? There is no way I'm taking advice from him."

At hole five, Steven shanked. Doug sent his ball into the wrong fairway. Ralph stepped up, took a practice swing, and then sent his ball straight down the fairway 300 yards. Wow! Perfect position. The next swing would put my team on the green and then Ralph managed to putt the ball in. Birdie.

The next four holes were much the same. Doug and Steven had basically forgotten how to play golf. Ralph now was carrying the weight of our team.

He made these incredible shots. Each time, he would grin slightly, tug at his cap, spit, and then walk back to the cart with his head tipped down. He didn't gloat. He just went on his humble way.

I started taking Ralph's advice. I widened my stance, concentrated, and swung with less might than before. Ping. The ball actually had some lift. It went straight. Maybe even 150 yards. It was the best drive of the day for me.

When I got back into the cart, I asked Ralph for more advice. He quietly gave little tidbits. Mostly he gave me a quick smile and said, "Atta girl," when I had done well.

By the eighteenth hole, Ralph and I were basically playing the game. Doug and Steven had lost their zest. There was the occasional incredible drive or the occasional lucky putt, but Ralph was consistent. He kept our team in the hunt. Ralph and I had even been able to strike up little conversations along the way.

When the game was over, I sat back in my cherished blue lawn chair. It had traveled to many a ball game, picnic, and camping trip. It had seen better days, but it was like an old friend with its tears and blemishes. The netting pocket where I kept my soda had torn, and I had to always double-check that the legs fully extended so it wouldn't dump me out. This faded old chair brought comfort.

In that comfortable old chair, I stared at Doug, Steven, and Ralph joking with others they knew. It occurred to me that Ralph had known what he was doing from the very beginning. I had a preconceived notion about what a great golfer should look like and he just didn't look the part, so I expected him to fail and I even found affirmation in the first few holes. I didn't look to Ralph as someone who could be coaching me or anyone else—that is, until I saw him pick up where the others had failed.

Over the course of the day, Ralph set the example as an influencer. He wasn't shy about standing shoulder-to-shoulder with the corporate guys. Here was someone who was understated and who never sought an ego boost. He never pushed his advice, but offered coaching in the most effective way—by modeling the right way to do it. This sounds familiar. Yet again, Dad's lesson to *be proud of where you come from* seems evident.

Things may come to those who wait, but only the things left by those who hustle.

– Anonymous

CHAPTER 10

Mistakes are Forgivable

This was a hard lesson for me. Mistakes are forgivable, but only if you admit them.

As my career started to bloom at the company, I was fortunate enough to add to my team. I hired a young man to work with me. I envisioned this highly productive, tandem-working relationship. We would build such a relationship where each one would be responsive to the other. We would play to each other's strengths. We would be the dynamic duo!

Sadly, that did not happen. After hiring the gentleman, I set out to create a vision for our team. I rented space away from the office so we could work without being distracted. Granted that space was different than what I had previously rented for the accounting team—we still weren't allowed back there. We could brainstorm and become this creative force that would transform the talent development process in our company.

Step one for our strategy meeting: define the mission for our team. I had notes on the history of the company, the few expectations from senior leadership, and even funnies from Harvard Business Review. (Really no reason for the funnies other than the fact that I enjoyed laughing.)

We started strong with agreeing on the current state of the business, but we clearly had very different opinions on what the future state looked like. I suggested very aggressive measures to support the business model. He also had great suggestions, but they were centered around human behavior without regard to the business. He quickly started correcting my vocabulary. He didn't see any value in walking through the steps of creating a team. He felt we would be more valuable if we just hit the pavement and corrected employee work behaviors.

Who was this guy and what did he do with the guy from the interview?

I challenged him. I told him I preferred we work through the process of identifying where we could make the most impact. Our discussions continued to disintegrate. Soon I found his brainstorming ideas to be irritating—almost combative. Finally I said, "We are done. I just cannot continue." That was hour two of our full-day planning retreat.

Days after that were spent avoiding each other. He felt it necessary to explore my reputation with others. They found that disturbing and came to me.

How dare he? My knee-jerk reaction was to say, "Listen, buddy, you are not through your probationary period yet!"

Thank goodness that thought didn't cross my lips. I considered everything that had happened. How much of that meeting was my fault? Did I allow my ego to get in the way? Did I prepare him correctly for that meeting, or did I just throw him into it and expect a miracle?

Sadly, I could find fault in all areas. My job was to be his supervisor. My job was to make him successful. And sadly, all I had succeeded at was alienating him and creating Death Valley between us.

I decided there was only one answer. I asked my team member to join me in a conference room, and I apologized. I apologized I got offended with being corrected. I apologized that we had a rough start. I wanted us to be a great team and work together. I assured him that I would be happy to take his feedback.

From that point, we did make greater strides to connect and form an alliance. Maybe he learned something from the experience. I am sure I learned much more, though, as a young manager. I wish I didn't have to learn from my mistakes in order to become an influential leader, but that seems to be my modus operandi.

I remembered that lawn mower incident from so many years earlier, when my dad hugged me and thanked me for taking responsibility and admitting my mistake. I felt comfort once again remembering my dad's advice: "The difference between good people and bad people is that good people will admit what they have done. Bad people will hide their mistakes." Although owning up to my mistakes was tough to do, this advice seemed to really pay off. Another of Dad's lessons strikes again—*Admit your mistakes.*

Peace begins with a smile.

–Mother Teresa

CHAPTER 11

Never Hype Your Serving Others

Tooting your own horn is not smart. I believe serving is incredibly personal and private. I recognize now how my dad's service to others influenced how I serve others. He modeled that serving is not something the server should hype. If so, it defeats the intention of serving.

I love to watch people. It's true entertainment for me. I especially enjoy observing generosity in others, particularly when the attempt is sublimated.

A coworker lost his only son in a car wreck one afternoon. The news was devastating. All of us who had children of similar age were terrified. We asked what everyone always asks in this situation: "What can we do for him?" There just simply is no great answer. I couldn't bear to imagine what he would want because it reminded me of my own child's mortality. What if that had been him?

Out of the blue, I heard someone comment about how they saw our chief financial officer, Greg, at my grieving coworker's house. He never asked us what we could do. He never gave any suggestions. He simply went home after work, loaded up his lawn mower, drove to my coworker's home, and mowed his neglected yard. He never said a word, but what an impact his efforts made. What a powerful example he set for us.

Serving others can be something as simple as including someone in that area of life where they are passionate. I have always had a passion for civic projects, and specifically economic development of rural towns. Dr. Rossi, general manager, called me one day and asked if I could serve, in his place, on a committee that was part of our local downtown development organization. In his mind, he was covering a commitment. In my mind, he just connected me to a passion. I was thankful he offered me an opportunity that fit my passion.

Serving others can also be joyful and it doesn't have to be complex. A fellow coworker, Molly, and I decided we needed to clean out a closet at work. The closet was full of sodas and water that were close to passing their use-by dates. We got a crazy idea. What if we iced them down and in the afternoon simply served others soda or water as a treat. Yes, we were cleaning, but the nearing expiration dates sparked an idea to use the drinks to thank everyone for their hard work.

We pushed our wobbly cooler full of iced drinks down the corridor and knocked on our first door. Dr. Halley was our first victim. We asked if he would prefer soda or water. He looked at both of us over those half-rimmed glasses that only really smart people wear and chuckled. He acted like he didn't understand English. Molly repeated the question. He accepted a soda. He sat there holding a cold can of soda in disbelief. Really? This is not a hard concept. And he has "Dr." in front of his name.

We moved on to the second person. Same response. Clearly, this is an activity that had never happened before.

We successfully delivered soda to the majority of the office, and more importantly, left behind smiles and chuckles. It was simple and fun.

Serving others can also take the form of meeting needs. We live on a small farm. My husband, Joe—or Farmer Joe for fun—loves machinery. The more, the better. The newer, the better. I often think these farmers get together over the fence row and show off their new buys.

Farmer Joe's guilty pleasure is his cherished chain saw. After every use, he dusts it, sharpens the teeth on the chain, and stores it in a majestic location high above other tools. Because he loves his chain saw so much, we always have ample firewood. I mean, you gotta be doing something with that tool. He's certainly not using it to create artwork.

He knew a widow who used wood heat in her home. We often pass her home, and we observed one day that there wasn't much of a supply of wood. He and our two sons loaded up the truck with two ricks of our wood, carefully choosing seasoned wood because it has had time to release the sap and burns more consistently. They drove to her house without notice and stacked the wood by her back door. She wasn't home, and they never said a word. But to see the generosity in their efforts made me proud. Dad would have been proud of them too.

Okay. The original model was:

> *Influence = Strength + Intelligence*
> *+ Go-To Person + Communication Skills*

Based on that model and the early escapades in my corporate career (and I only mentioned a few here, but my therapist feels it's healthy for me), I wasn't sure if I would ever have a chance of influencing anyone on this planet. I had not proven myself to be an assertive or highly intelligent person. Was I really a go-to person with a high-level of commitment? Did I possess those incredible communication skills?

Becoming influential seemed a bit out of reach for someone like me.

What I have noticed through these years since my early attempts to become an influencer is that a different model is actually more effective. Interestingly enough, it is the same model my dad taught me from the farm:

> *Influence = Be Proud of Where you Came From*
> *+ Admit Mistakes + Communicate*
> *+ Laugh at Yourself + Serve Others*

Ralph, the redneck golfer, taught me a valuable lesson on being proud of where you come from at any given time or in any situation—a lesson I enjoyed and embrace today.

Admitting mistakes only positions those around you to embrace you more. It also allows you to graciously recover and learn from them.

Learning to communicate was a hard-learned lesson that has served me well. Sometimes that involved swallowing pride and communicating the fact I am wrong. Sometimes that involves explaining to police officers the reality of a situation. And sometimes it is as simple as listening to someone else explain how you can improve.

The fact that I could laugh about things like the hostage situation at the bank, mistakenly stealing a van from the airport, or that a vice president in our company knows my pants size, all made me more approachable. Being approachable has opened numerous doors in my career.

Serving others, just as Dad suggested, is simple and enjoyable. It's there that I've found a way to live my passion in the community as well as in my personal and professional life.

We are the creative force of our life, and through our own decisions rather than our conditions, if we carefully learn to do certain things, we can accomplish those goals.

– Stephen Covey

CHAPTER 12

What Will Your Legacy Be?

How do you know if you really learned anything in life, or what your legacy will be? I think you have to see evidence of your personal purpose and then the passion in your evidence. For example, my dad has a building named after him. Since he was first and foremost a farmer, rest assured he didn't buy his way on the brick. The name was a gift of honor and tribute to a man who lived through character and spirit to promote those things dear to him.

So what is my purpose?

I have two boys. Raising boys on a farm can at times be stressful. My husband takes great pride in teaching the boys to work and to share his hobbies of hunting and fishing. I take great pride in teaching my boys the traditions I grew up with as well, like participating in the cattle shows.

As I mentioned earlier, farm life includes teaching young people to drive equipment very early. This came easy for our older boy, Webb. He was a natural—at least in driving. Abiding by speed limits was another story.

It eventually came time for Tater (his real name is Wade—we did not name him after a carbohydrate) to learn to drive. My husband taught him the basics. He taught him how to start the farm truck, put it into gear, and then how to stop and park. It was a good day. Tater was feeling proud of himself, as he was getting to do something his older brother could do.

Tater decided to surprise his grandparents, who lived down the dirt road from our house, with a visit. I knew he was driving across the pasture so I called Mom to warn her and basically ruin the surprise.

Hours passed. I heard Tater return. He walked into the house with his head hung low. I quickly asked why he looked so depressed. Tater asked me to follow him outside.

I quietly followed only to see why he was so depressed. The truck was sitting there with a giant dent in the fender. Tater looked up at me and explained he had made a mistake and turned the corner too sharp. To make matters worse, he hit the gas instead of the brake and then hit the gate.

He had tears welling up in his eyes and had taken a three-point stance, ready for the worst. I looked at him and said, "The difference between good people and bad people are that good people will admit what they have done. Bad people will hide their mistakes."

I looked him in the eye and said, "Mistakes happen. We just have to fix what we can, and own what we can't." I told him those words came from a great and wise man, who had the same life in his eyes as Tater does, and same crooked grin. Then I advised him never to forget those words and never let the spirit drain from his eyes.

I thanked him for admitting that he dented the truck. I gave him a hug and told him we needed to go look at the gate. A smile ran across his face. He said, "The gate is a casualty. It didn't survive."

In early 2013, I had the pleasure of working with a small committee of agriculturalists on the topic of sustainability through poultry. The focus was to find a way to educate young consumers on the need for solid and responsible agriculture methods.

We spent hours brainstorming ways to engage them, but couldn't develop any practical solutions. We arrived at an epiphany: we don't know how.

We decided to create a contest to challenge the FFA chapters in the state of Arkansas to engage their students and send us a media product we can use.

Later that summer, I took the stage at the Arkansas Vocational Agriculture Teacher In-Service Training to present the idea for the contest. I started my talk with, "The last time I was here, I stood on this stage and participated in the extemporaneous contest. And I lost!" Being able to admit a loss is a great attribute. The FFA is very competitive and encouraging, so I was in my safe place.

One of the teachers quickly asked me what school I represented. I replied, "Lincoln. My maiden name is Webb." I was proud of where I came from and wanted to give my dad some recognition. But you see, he was more than a man. Not only was he my beloved father, he was also a former FFA Advisor. A man who, through character and spirit, gifted so many people in Arkansas opportunities they might not have enjoyed without him. And I knew that. We lost my dad to Alzheimer's in May 2012. And everyone in that room knew that.

At that moment, the most incredible experience of my life happened. The teachers all started applauding and even stood up. It wasn't to applaud me or to applaud the contest. They were applauding my name—the name of the man who had made such an impact on them, the state, and the FFA organization.

This was evidence. It was evidence that I am the daughter of a legacy. It was evidence of his influence on the lives of every one of those teachers. It was evidence that he impacted the students as well as the community I grew up in. And of course, my life is evidence of that same inspiring influence as I strive to live and teach those simple principles he taught me:

> *Be proud of where you come from*
>
> *Admit your mistakes*
>
> *Communicate*
>
> *Laugh at yourself*
>
> *Serve others*
>
> *Live with purpose and passion*

Here is my question to you. Fourteen months after you pass from this earth, will people applaud your name?

If you even questioned that question, then it's time to take charge of your life and live it with legacy in mind.

Be kind, for everyone you meet is fighting a hard battle.

–Ian MacLaren

About the Author

Sheila Pierson has a passion for helping coworkers and friends succeed. Sheila has a fifteen-year accomplished track record of coaching for success, as well as inspiring others to lead teams through chaos into achieving remarkable results.

From the classroom to the boardroom to the civic hall, her message is clear and simple: live toward your legacy.

Sheila uses her Southern charm to entertain while mastering the art of storytelling to reach audiences and individuals.

She grew up in northwest Arkansas and holds a Bachelor of Science degree in Agriculture Business and a Master of Science degree in Agriculture Economics from the great hog nation, aka the University of Arkansas.

Sheila and her family are currently the fourth generation of family farmers to operate an Angus cow calf farm.